Pale

by
**Janet
Schulman**

illustrated by
**Meilo
So**

Alfred A. Knopf
New York

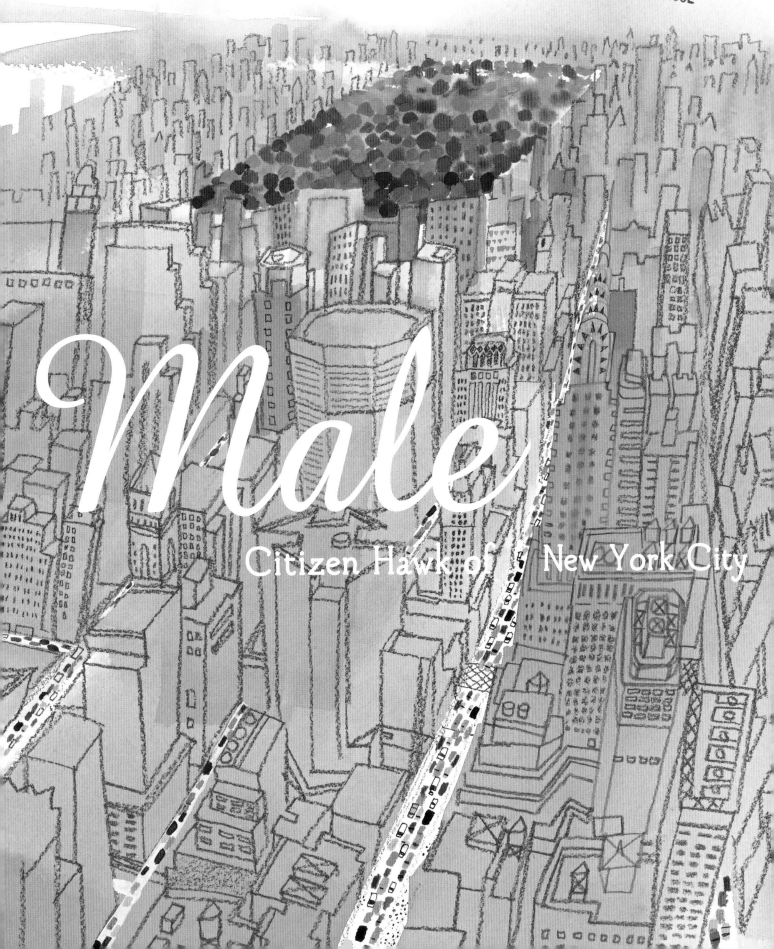

Male

Citizen Hawk of New York City

One crisp autumn day in 1991, a red-tailed hawk flew across the Hudson River from New Jersey. He flew over smokestacks, skyscrapers, and ant-like traffic to a rectangular oasis smack in the center of New York City. The hawk soared above Central Park. He surveyed the trees, the small lakes, the tall buildings on all four sides. And with his keen hawk vision, he spotted lunch—so many plump pigeons and rats and squirrels!

Red-tailed hawks often stop for a few days and sometimes spend the winter in Central Park, but they are shy birds and eventually fly away to quiet farmlands or wooded mountains.

This bird was different. He liked what he saw, and he stayed.

Birdwatchers in Central Park liked what they saw, too. A spectacular red-tailed hawk! He loomed large in the sky with a wingspan of four feet. And his unusual coloring—beige rather than dark brown, with breast and belly feathers nearly pure white—made him easy to track.

The birdwatchers named him Pale Male and kept notes on him daily. Pale Male hung around the park the way a teenager hangs out at a mall. He dive-bombed tasty pigeons and rats at their litter-can snack bars. He chased after ducks and was spotted terrorizing squirrels, seemingly just for the fun of it. As red-tailed hawks go, he *was* a teenager. His brown tail feathers gave it away. These hawks don't get their distinctive reddish brown tail feathers until they are mature, about two years old.

Pale Male thrived in his new home. And the birders were thrilled when he began courting another redtail. Day after day they performed an aerial ballet of circling and swooping in unison over the park until, young as he was, Pale Male won her as his mate.

In March the two hawks began building a nest in a tree near a baseball diamond on the Great Lawn. This was the first time that hawks had nested in the park since it opened in 1858.

But Pale Male and his mate were inexperienced builders. Their nest fell apart a month later.

Undaunted, the two hawks immediately began building another nest in a tree near East 70th Street. This time it was not poor construction but location that did them in. The tree they chose had housed a crows' nest the year before. Crows are natural enemies of hawks, and the crows of Central Park responded with unusual ferocity when they saw hawks nesting in "their" tree. Flocks of screaming black birds harassed the two hawks every time they left their nest. Finally Pale Male's mate became so disoriented that she slammed into a high-rise at East 73rd Street. Witnesses called the Audubon Society. Her wing was badly broken, and she was taken to a hawk rescue center in New Jersey.

The birdwatchers wondered what would happen to Pale Male now. They waited and watched, and the following winter Pale Male, now sporting a flashy red tail, found a new mate. In March they began building a nest. This nest would be different. This time Pale Male moved his residence to a ledge above a top-floor window at 927 Fifth Avenue, one of New York City's most exclusive apartment buildings.

Bird experts had never heard of a red-tailed hawk with its nest on a building in the center of a bustling city. Maybe Pale Male wasn't too smart.

But soon they saw that this bird was actually very smart. Metal spikes had been embedded in the ledge above the window to keep pigeons away. By forcing sticks and branches between these spikes, the hawks made a nest that could withstand hurricane winds. An ornate cornice hanging over the ledge provided protection from the elements. The building was just across the street from some of Pale Male's favorite hunting grounds. And the view of the park from the twelfth floor was spectacular! New Yorkers couldn't ask for a better address. Neither could Pale Male.

As spring progressed, Pale Male and his mate took turns sitting on three eggs. Ignoring window washers and wailing fire engines and honking horns below, they sat and they sat. And birders watched and waited. The eggs should have hatched by late April or early May. Finally in June it became obvious that the eggs were not going to hatch. The hawks' small fan club was disappointed.

But later in June their sadness turned to shock when they discovered that the building management of 927 Fifth Avenue had removed the nest. Residents had complained about bird droppings, feathers, and the remains of dead animals sometimes falling to the sidewalk in front of their building. The wealthy New Yorkers who lived there did not consider these messy hawks to be the kind of neighbors they wanted.

Some hawk experts thought that Pale Male would find a new nest site. But Pale Male would not be evicted. He and his mate returned in the spring and built a new nest exactly where the old one had been.

This time the building management left it alone, thanks to a stern warning from the U.S. Fish and Wildlife Service, threatening substantial fines. Hawks were protected under the Migratory Bird Treaty Act of 1918. Destroying their nests was a serious violation.

And a year later, in April 1995, the hawks' perseverance was rewarded! Three fluffy white chicks were born in New York City.

The hawk watchers of Central Park were ecstatic. From early morning until nightfall they gathered around the model-boat pond to get the best view of the nest. They watched Mom and Dad Hawk tend their babies and talked about the chicks like proud new aunts and uncles.

New Yorkers on their way to work or out for a stroll wondered what celebrity these people could be spying on with their binoculars and telescopes. The enthusiastic hawk watchers were always happy to point out the nest, and it was the rare person who was not surprised and delighted to discover a family of hawks making a home in the city.

News of the hawks spread, and soon New Yorkers who had never been birdwatchers before were stopping by the model-boat pond to see what they could see. The hawks were becoming Fifth Avenue's most admired celebrities!

By June the chicks had grown almost as large as their parents. Gone was their baby down—now they had flight feathers. They began jumping up and down in the nest and flapping their wings in preparation for their first flights. In the wild their nest would have been in a tree with branches to hop down to until they got the hang of flying.

The birders were worried. Would these city hawks survive that scary first flight with nothing but cement and asphalt below them? The first fledgling took off with a big hop and then began flapping his wings madly like an oversized sparrow until he landed—awkwardly but safely—on the roof of an apartment building several blocks up Fifth Avenue.

The fledgling spent the day half-flying, half-hopping from balcony to balcony until Pale Male gave his brave baby a first lesson in how to fly like a self-respecting hawk.

The fledgling watched his father soar over the Metropolitan Museum of Art and circle back with scarcely a flap of his wings. The novice caught on and proudly flapped—slowly— back to his nest, just in time for dinner.

Within a few days all three fledglings had abandoned their cramped nest for the trees of Central Park.

Each spring more and more fans of the hawks came out to watch Pale Male and his mate renovate their nest with new twigs and leaves. And there was always a great celebration when new chicks hatched. The birders watched the hardworking parents ferry home pigeons, rats, and occasionally a squirrel or a songbird from their well-stocked Central Park meat market. Even after fledglings left the nest, they would stay under the protection of their parents for several months. Pale Male would always respond to their hungry cries with some meat. He would chase off those pesky crows and let his hawklets know that the blue jay bullies couldn't really harm them. This good dad was once observed helping his hawklets learn to catch rodents by dropping a live mouse near one of them.

Over the next nine years the hawks
would rear twenty-three chicks. And
a CBS News commentator actually
nominated Pale Male for Father of the
Year! Life in the big city was good for the
hawks. Little did Pale Male know that his
greatest challenge was yet to come.

In December 2004 the owners of 927 Fifth Avenue removed Pale Male's nest along with the anti-pigeon spikes that anchored it. Most of the tenants had been irked for years that they couldn't legally get rid of the hawks. Then in 2003, during a time when many conservation and wildlife laws were being relaxed by President George W. Bush's administration, the Migratory Bird Treaty was changed. It now permitted destruction of nests as long as there were no eggs or chicks in the nest. Hawks lay their eggs in March and the chicks fledge in June. In December Pale Male's nest was empty. The owners of the hawk building were quick to take advantage of the new law.

All of New York heard about it in a flash. Television newscasts told all of America. The news traveled abroad in Japanese, French, Arabic, and other languages. New Yorkers and nature lovers everywhere were stunned. Taking down the nest seemed like such a heartless act coming from people living in their own well-feathered nests.

The dedicated birdwatchers and the Audubon Society immediately organized protests across Fifth Avenue from the hawk building. Every day more and more people joined the chorus, chanting "Bring back the nest," "Bring back the spikes," "Shame! Shame!" Two protesters dressed as birds urged cars on Fifth Avenue to "Honk 4 Hawks." Taxis, cars, and city buses honked. Trucks let out ear-piercing blasts of their air horns. Even fire trucks let loose their sirens.

Pale Male circled high above the protesters, silently watching.

NYC ♥ Kids ♥ Pale Male

BRING BACK THE SPIKES

HONK 4 HAWKS

POM

After a week with hundreds of protesters blocking the sidewalk, with traffic slowed to a crawl, and with constant, relentless noise, the building owners backed down. The publicity had been terrible for them! The Audubon Society and the U.S. Fish and Wildlife Service finally persuaded the owners to reinstall the anti-pigeon spikes and to construct an apron, or cradle, below the nest to catch the hawks' garbage.

The hawks kept a wary eye on the ledge until the spikes and apron were installed and the workers' scaffolding was finally removed. Within minutes the hawk couple began bringing new twigs to the ledge. They would rebuild their home and start over again.

The red-tailed hawks had brought great joy to the people of New York, and now the people of New York returned the favor. The hawks were welcome to stay at 927 Fifth Avenue as long as they wanted.

They were true-blue New Yorkers—tough, resourceful, and determined to make it in the city. New Yorkers loved them for bringing a touch of the wild and a respect for nature to a teeming urban landscape.

Pale Male gave the city another gift as well. In the spring of 2005, some fifteen blocks south of Pale Male's nest, another redtail and his mate set up housekeeping. They built their nest on a ledge on the thirty-fifth floor of Trump Parc on Central Park South and hatched two chicks. Birdwatchers believe that this light-colored hawk with a taste for high-rise apartments is a son of Pale Male. Junior is his name.

And so the legacy of Pale Male, the majestic hawk who is different, lives on.

Long live Pale Male!

Author's Note

I first learned of Pale Male in 1995 during an Audubon bird walk in Central Park. On that bird walk I also learned that Central Park is one of the fourteen best places in America to birdwatch, ranking right up there with Yosemite National Park. Two hundred seventy-five different species have been spotted in the park, ninety-five on just that one April day I was there.

As the American Northeast becomes an almost solid belt of housing developments, shopping malls, and parking lots, more and more migrating birds are stopping off to rest and refuel at this green zone. Native wildlife is also affected by the shrinking rural areas surrounding New York City. With less open country and less food, many hawks do not survive their first winter. Some believe that Pale Male was driven off his natural habitat by adult hawks protecting their territory and that he was forced to go far afield to find a place with ample food and no adult hawks to harass him.

After the Audubon birders pointed out Pale Male's eight-foot-wide nest atop the ritzy Fifth Avenue apartment building, I would stop by each spring to see if there were chicks. And when there were, it always seemed like a miracle that these naturally shy wild birds could adapt so well to America's noisiest, busiest steel-and-concrete city. Pale Male has had four mates—First Love, Chocolate, Blue, and his mate since 2002, Lola. Only when his mate was killed or seriously injured did he take a new mate. He has now won the status of a true New York celebrity: his building is pointed out by tour-bus operators.

Central Park, with its 843 acres, is large enough to support a number of hawk families. In addition to Pale Male and the hawk called Junior, a redtail and his mate have reared two chicks in their nest perched on the limestone shoulders of St. Andrew on the Cathedral of St. John the Divine, just north of Central Park. These hawks and several others frequently spotted near the tennis courts may be offspring of Pale Male. And so might the two redtails that I frequently see in Riverside Park, about a half mile west of Central Park. Red-tailed hawks like to set up housekeeping not too far from where they hatched.

New York City's parks are much more than a refuge for millions of New Yorkers. Besides the many birds (including a wild turkey) in Central Park, I've seen rabbits, frogs, turtles, and countless squirrels. Raccoons, woodchucks, and snakes also live there, not to mention many different species of butterflies. And in 2005 a coyote was found hiding out there. Taking a walk through Central Park is always a nature lover's delight. And if you are lucky, you may even see Pale Male!

Janet Schulman

Janet Schulman
March 2008

For my editor, Nancy Siscoe –J.S.
For Max Aaron Hanks –M.S.

The author gratefully acknowledges the work of Marie Winn. She was the first to report the facts about Pale Male's life in her *Wall Street Journal* articles and in her book *Red-Tails in Love*. These sources provided much of the story told in *Pale Male: Citizen Hawk of New York City*.

Selected Sources for Further Study:
Red-Tails in Love by Marie Winn. New York: Pantheon Books, 1998; Vintage Books, 1999, 2005.
Birds of Central Park, text and photographs by Cal Vornberger. New York: Harry N. Abrams, 2005.
Pale Male, DVD directed by Frederic Lillien and narrated by Joanne Woodward. New York:
   PBS Thirteen-WNET, 2003.
www.mariewinn.com
www.palemale.com

THIS IS A BORZOI BOOK PUBLISHED BY ALFRED A. KNOPF

Text copyright © 2008 by Janet Schulman
Illustrations copyright © 2008 by Meilo So

Published in the United States by Alfred A. Knopf, an imprint of Random House Children's Books,
a division of Random House, Inc., New York.

KNOPF, BORZOI BOOKS, and the colophon are registered trademarks of Random House, Inc.

www.randomhouse.com/kids

Educators and librarians, for a variety of teaching tools,
visit us at www.randomhouse.com/teachers

Library of Congress Cataloging-in-Publication Data
Schulman, Janet.
Pale Male : citizen hawk of New York City / by Janet Schulman ; illustrated by Meilo So.
   p. cm.
ISBN 978-0-375-84558-1 (trade) — ISBN 978-0-375-94558-8 (lib. bdg.)
1. Red-tailed hawk—New York (State)—New York—Anecdotes—Juvenile literature.
I. So, Meilo, ill. II. Title.
QL696.F32S38 2008
598.9'44—dc22
2007014661

The illustrations in this book were created on Arches cold press watercolor paper
with watercolor inks and colored pencils.

MANUFACTURED IN MALAYSIA
March 2008
10 9 8 7 6 5 4
First Edition